Presented to:

_____

Date:

_____

BOYS

LIFE ADVENTURE

BIBLE

Storybook

BOYS LIFE ADVENTURE BIBLE Storybook

David Horton
Illustrated by Dennis Edwards

Published in
Association with

BAKER
A DIVISION OF
Baker Book House Co

CONTENTS

A World Of Wonder 8

A Companion For Adam 15

The Blame Game 22

A Really, Really Big Boat 29

Take Your Pick 36

A Test Of Love 43

By Hook Or By Crook 50

Joseph's Jealous Brothers 57

Joseph Runs Into Trouble 64

A Surprise Reunion .71

The Baby In The Basket-Boat 78

A Fiery Job Offer 85

God Gets Pharaoh's Attention 92

Food From Heaven 99

God's Rules 106

Jethro's Good Advice 113

God's Explorers 120

Moses' Big Mistake 127

A Voice In The Night 134

Big Enough 141

Best Friends 148

Fire And Water 155

The Oil Business 162

The Miracle Bath 169

The Youngest King 176
A Job To Do 183
Esther's Dangerous Mission .190
Problems And More Problems 196
Daniel's Dangerous Prayer 203
The Giant Fish 210
No Room 217
Telling The Good News 224
Satan's Tricks 231
Through The Roof 238
The Miracle Picnic 245
The Runaway Son 252
The Good Neighbor 259
One Out Of Ten 266
Little Man, Big Heart 273
The Master's Money 280
Cleaning Up God's House 287
Washing Dirty Feet 294
A One-Man Parade 301
The Greatest Love 308
Surprise In The Garden 315
Gone But Not Forgotten 322
Just The Facts, Please 329
Outdoor School 336
The Great Escape 343
Singing In Jail 350

A World of
WONDER

Before God started his work, the world was not a pretty place. There were no flowers, or trees, or animals of any kind. It was just wet, empty, and very dark.

But God decided to change all that. He began by creating light so it would only be dark at night.

The next day, God created miles and miles of beautiful blue sky. On the third day, he began moving things around. Some places he filled with water, and he called them "seas." The dry places he called "land." Then he created grass, and flowers, and all sorts of plants and trees to cover the land

God created some special lights to brighten the world on the fourth day. The lights made it easier to tell time, too. The warm sun lit up the day. At night, the moon glowed and the stars twinkled.

On the fifth day, God created fish, whales, dolphins, crabs, and all kinds of creatures to swim in the seas.

Then he created robins, eagles, parakeets, flamingos and lots of other birds to roam the skies.

God started the sixth day by creating all sorts of animals: bears, moose, elephants, kangaroos, zebras, and more. He made big animals, small animals, farm animals, and wild animals.

Before the day was over, God created people, too. And he put them in charge of everything else he had made.

But on the seventh day, God decided to rest. He had worked hard to create the world and everything in it. And it was all very good!

Based on Genesis 1

Making a Man of God

A MAN OF GOD
WORSHIPS THE CREATOR.

God made the world a very special place. One way we can show God how much we love him is to take good care of the world he made. Can you think of some ways to take care of God's world?

Can you count all the things God created? Which is your favorite?

The next time you go outside, tell God "thank you" for creating so many wonderful things.

Coaching Tips

Take a walk outside and observe the grandeur, variety, and detail in God's creation. Your backyard, a city park, a field, beach, or forest—each can provide ample evidence of God's creative genius. Encourage your young man's curiosity about the world around him—and about the God who made it.

A Verse to Remember

IN THE BEGINNING, GOD CREATED THE
HEAVENS AND THE EARTH.
GENESIS 1:1

A Companion for Adam

Adam was the very first person God made. He lived in a beautiful garden filled with plants, trees, and all kinds of animals. There was even a river running through it. God gave Adam the important job of taking care of the garden!

But Adam was the only person on earth, and he
was lonely. "It's not good for you to be alone,"
said God. "I'll make a companion to help you."

So God showed Adam all the animals and birds
he had made to see what he thought. He even let
Adam give them all names.

Adam named horses, cows, dogs, and cats, as well as zebras, elephants, lions, and hippopotamuses. And when he finished the animals, he named all the birds, like robins, eagles, owls, and parakeets.

"I like all the different animals and birds," said Adam. "Some of them will be good helpers, too. But I still feel lonely. I need a companion who is more like me."

God knew just what Adam needed. So he told Adam to take a nice long nap. While Adam was asleep, God took out one of his ribs and used it to make a woman.

When Adam woke up, he could hardly believe his eyes! He called the woman Eve, and he knew right away that she was someone special.

"She is a part of me," he said happily. "Now I have someone to share my life with. And I don't have to be lonely anymore."

Based on Genesis 2

Making a Man of God

A man of God
values others.

Adam had everything a man could ask for: friendship with God, a perfect place to live, a great job. But God knew that something-or rather someone-very important was missing in Adam's life. He knew that Adam needed someone to share his life with. Friendships and family members are very important. So God made Eve. And Adam was glad he did!

Can you think of ways you can show your family, your friends-or even people you don't know very well-how important they are?

Remember to thank God for the special people in your life. Everyone is important to God, and they should be important to us, too.

Coaching Tips

Tell your young man about your courtship. What do you value about this special companion God provided for you?

Make sure your children see how much you value people. Do you treat others with respect and dignity, regardless of gender, race, or creed?

A Verse to Remember

So God created people in his own image . . . male and female he created them.
Genesis 1:27

THE BLAME GAME

Adam and Eve had a wonderful life in the special garden God made. They didn't have to worry about buying shoes or new clothes. They didn't have to make any house payments. They never had to buy groceries. And they didn't have to worry about going on a diet; God told them they could eat anything in the garden they wanted! Well, almost anything.

"You may not eat the fruit from one special tree," God told them. "If you do, you will die."

So Adam and Eve stayed away from the special tree that was in the center of the garden. They took care of the garden each day and everything was fine.

But one day an evil snake came to visit Eve. He convinced her to eat the fruit from the special tree.

"It tastes delicious!" Eve told Adam. "Here, try some."

Adam tried some, too. And it was delicious.

Later that day, Adam and Eve heard God coming. They both felt guilty about disobeying him, so they hid in the trees.

"Adam," called God. "Why are you hiding? Did you
eat some of the fruit I told you not to eat?"

"Yes," Adam admitted, "but it was Eve's fault.
She gave it to me."

"It wasn't my fault," said Eve. "The snake tricked
me."

But God wasn't interested in their excuses.
"Because you disobeyed me," he said, "you may no
longer live in my garden."

Adam and Eve's perfect life was over. From that
day on they would have to work hard just to get
enough to eat.

Based on Genesis 3

Making a Man of God

A MAN OF GOD DOESN'T BLAME
HIS MISTAKES ON OTHERS.

Adam and Eve tried to blame their
problems on someone else. They both
made bad choices. And they had no one
to blame but themselves.

Have you ever blamed someone else
for something you did? Have you ever
said, "It's not my fault" when you made a
mistake?

Coaching Tips

Tell your child that everyone makes mistakes. God loves us no matter what, but he wants us to be honest about our behavior.

Explain how blaming others can damage our relationships and keep us from developing godly character.

Does your family hear you blaming your boss, co-workers, parents, or spouse for your own mistakes or failures? Let them see that you accept responsibility for your own actions.

A Verse to Remember

I CONFESSED ALL MY SINS TO YOU AND STOPPED TRYING TO HIDE THEM.
PSALM 32:5

A REALLY, REALLY
BIG BOAT

"**I** want you to help me build a big boat," Noah told his three sons. "We have to be ready when God sends the flood."

Shem wondered if it was a waste of time. People said his dad was crazy, talking about a flood that would cover the whole earth.

"Who ever heard of such a thing," some laughed. "It's ridiculous!"

"And he wants to fill his boat with animals," joked others. "Phew! What a smell!"

Shem had to admit that it seemed pretty strange. But he knew his dad always tried to do what God told him, no matter what other people said.

"I'll help you, Father," Shem said at last, and his brothers agreed. The boat was so big that by the time it was done, Shem and his brothers were married.

As the sky grew dark with clouds, the boys helped Noah get the animals, birds—even insects—bringing them into the boat two at a time. With eight people and too many animals to count, they were glad the boat was extra large!

After they were all safely inside, the rain began to fall.
It didn't stop for forty days. The water got so deep
the boat floated over the mountaintops! Months went
by, and little by little, the water disappeared.

When Shem and his family finally got out on dry
land, they had been on the boat for a whole year!

"Thank you, God, for saving us from the flood," said
Noah, Shem and the rest of their family.

Based on Genesis 6-8

Making a Man of God

A MAN OF GOD IS OBEDIENT.

Sometimes it is hard to obey when people make fun of us or the things we believe. What would have happened if Shem had listened to other people instead of Noah?

Can you think of a time when you were tempted to disobey? What happened?

Remember, obeying God isn't always easy, but it is always right.

Coaching Tips

Tell about a time you faced a choice between obedience and popularity with your friends. What did you choose? What were the consequences of the choice you made?

Set an example for your young man by obeying rules and laws, even when others don't. Let him see that you are not swayed by popular opinion.

Remind your young man of a time when he obeyed you. Tell him how proud you were of him.

Reassure your young man that God forgives us, even when we make the wrong choice.

A Verse to Remember

CHILDREN, OBEY YOUR PARENTS.
EPHESIANS 6:1

TAKE YOUR
PICK

God promised Abraham that he would give him a new land. So Abraham took all his tents, his money, and his farm animals—everything he owned—and started traveling. He knew God would show him where to go.

Abraham told his nephew Lot that he could come,
too. Lot had many cows and sheep and tents of his
own. They traveled a long way together.

After a while, Abraham could see that living so
close was not a good idea. His workers kept
arguing with Lot's workers over who needed the
most grass.

The animals were not getting enough to eat because there wasn't enough grass to feed them all. Abraham didn't like all the arguing. Lot was part of his family.

Then Abraham had an idea. "Why don't we move a little away from each other?" he asked Lot. "Choose any piece of land you like. If you want to move away, I will stay here. If you want to stay, I will move away."

Lot liked Uncle Abraham's idea. He looked around at all the land in the area. Some of it was good and some of it wasn't. Finally, he chose the very best land, with the most grass and water, for himself. His animals would have plenty to eat there.

"Good-bye, Uncle Abraham," said Lot. And he packed up his tents and moved away.

Abraham knew Lot had taken the best land. But he wasn't worried. He knew that God would take care of him.

Based on Genesis 13

Making a Man of God

A MAN OF GOD IS NOT SELFISH.

Abraham could have kept the best land for himself, couldn't he? After all, he was the uncle, and Lot was probably much younger. But Abraham didn't have to be selfish to get what he needed. God promised to take care of him, and Abraham knew God would keep his promise. That made it easier to let Lot choose first.

Sometimes it's hard to share with your brother or sister, or even a friend, isn't it? Next time you have something to share, try letting someone else choose first.

Coaching Tip

Selfishness isn't just for kids, is it? Often we adults use our age or our standing as parents or grandparents to justify getting what we want. Why not set a memorable example? Give up something to which you normally feel entitled, in favor of your young man. It will be a lesson in unselfishness he won't soon forget.

Lot thought only of himself, and ended up homeless and in shame years later.

A Verse to Remember

DON'T BE SELFISH.
PHILIPPIANS 2:3

A Test of
LOVE

Father sure seems quiet today, thought Isaac as he trudged up the hill.

Isaac was an only child, and today he and his dad were hiking up a mountain to offer a sacrifice to God. Since he was young and strong, Isaac carried the firewood on his shoulders. But something didn't seem quite right.

"Father," Isaac said, "we have everything we need for the fire, but didn't we forget a lamb to sacrifice?"

"God will provide a lamb, son," replied his father. And they kept climbing higher up the mountain.

When they got to the top, Isaac helped gather stones to make an altar. He was starting to get worried. Where will we find a lamb way up here? he wondered. Why didn't Father bring one with him?

Suddenly, his father began tying him up.

"Father! What are you doing?" Isaac was really scared now. He didn't understand. Was he going to be the sacrifice? Before he knew it he was lying on top of the stone altar. But just when

he thought it was all over, he heard a strange voice:

"Don't hurt the boy," an angel told Isaac's dad. "I can see now that you love God even more than your only son. You will be blessed because you obeyed me."

Just then they noticed a ram caught in the bushes nearby. God had provided a sacrifice after all! Isaac felt so relieved, and he could tell his dad felt the same way.

Based on Genesis 22

Making a Man of God

A MAN OF GOD LOVES GOD MOST OF ALL.

God was giving Isaac's dad, Abraham, a test to see who he loved the most. Abraham didn't want to hurt Isaac, but he loved God more than anything—or anyone. He knew God would take care of everything, no matter what. And he was right!

Is there anything in your life that is more important to you than God? It might be something you own, or a special friend, or your parents. Could you give up that thing or person if that's what God wanted?

Coaching Tips

Tell about a time when something in your life seemed more important than God.

What did you do about it? How did God meet your need?

Make a point of assuring your young man of your deep, enduring love for him. Let him know that even though God wants our first love, he also wants us to love each other.

A Verse to Remember

AND YOU MUST LOVE THE LORD YOUR GOD WITH ALL YOUR HEART, ALL YOUR SOUL, AND ALL YOUR STRENGTH.

DEUTERONOMY 6:5

By Hook or by Crook

Jacob and Esau were twins. Esau was born first, and he was very hairy. When he grew up he loved to be outdoors and he became a great hunter. Jacob had very smooth skin, and he preferred to stay at home. He learned to be a very good cook.

One day, while Jacob was busy cooking, Esau came in from hunting. "I'm starving!" he said, all out of breath. "Give me some of that delicious stew you're making."

"I'll give you some stew," said Jacob, "but only if you give me your birthright."

Now in those days, the oldest son got more rights and privileges than all the other children. This was called a birthright.

"What good will my birthright do me if I starve to death?" said Esau. "You can have it. Just give me some food!" Jacob smiled to himself. He had just tricked his brother out of his most valuable possession, but Esau didn't seem to care.

Later their father called for Esau so he could give him a special blessing. When Jacob heard about it, he put on a disguise and went to see his father first.

"Who's there?" called his father, who was getting old and blind.

"It's me, Esau," said Jacob, doing his best imitation of his brother. And so their father blessed Jacob instead of Esau.

"That's the second time he's tricked me!" shouted Esau when he found out. "Now I'm going to kill him!"

Jacob was afraid. So he ran away from home and never returned.

Based on Genesis 25 & 27

Making a Man of God

A MAN OF GOD

VALUES HONESTY.

Jacob had a guilty conscience because he had been dishonest. It was years before he could face his brother Esau again. Even then, he worried that Esau was still angry with him.

If Jacob had played fair with his brother, would he have had anything to worry about?

Do you try to trick others sometimes, in order to get what you want? How do you think that makes them feel?

Coaching Tips

Tell about a time someone dealt with you dishonestly. Let your young man know how sad, angry, or disappointed you felt. Tell about a time when you were dishonest and what the results were.

Help your young man understand how quickly trust is broken by dishonesty or deceit. Let him know that you will always tell him the truth—and will expect it in return.

A Verse to Remember

IT IS BETTER TO BE POOR AND GODLY
THAN RICH AND DISHONEST.
PROVERBS 16:8

JOSEPH'S
JEALOUS
BROTHERS

Jacob had a very large family. But of his twelve sons, he loved Joseph the best. "I have a gift for you—a special coat," he told Joseph, when his son was seventeen.

"Thank you, Father," said Joseph. "It's the most beautiful coat I've ever seen. I think I'll show it to my brothers."

But his brothers weren't at all happy for Joseph. "Father always spoils you," they grumbled. "He never gives us any special gifts."

Then Joseph had some dreams. In one dream, he and his brothers were gathering grain into bundles. Joseph's bundle stood up and all the other bundles bowed down to it.

In another dream, the sun, moon, and
stars all bowed down to him. When he
told his brothers about the dreams, they
were furious. "Do you think you're our
ruler?" they shouted.

One day Joseph went to find his brothers, who were out watching the sheep. "Here comes the dreamer," the brothers said when they saw Joseph coming. "He's nothing but trouble. We should kill him." So they grabbed Joseph and threw him in a deep pit. He begged them not to, but they wouldn't listen.

Finally, Joseph's brothers did take him
out of the pit—and sold him to some
traveling traders. Then they told their
father that wild animals had killed
Joseph.

But in spite of all that happened,
God didn't forget about Joseph.

Based on Genesis 37

Making a Man of God

A MAN OF GOD IS NOT
RULED BY JEALOUSY.

Why were Joseph's brothers so jealous they wanted to hurt him? Maybe they forgot that everyone is important to God, whether we like them or not.

Have you ever been jealous of someone—a brother, a sister, a friend? Did it make you want to hurt that person, or say bad things about them? What should you do when you feel that way?

Coaching Tips

Do you set an example by thinking and speaking well of siblings, co-workers, and others—even those who seem to be treated better than you?

Help your young man to understand that life isn't always "fair," and that everyone does not receive equal treatment, as much as we might wish it were so. Explain that God's love, the most important thing in life, is freely available to everyone, no matter who they are. Since all people are important to God, we should treat them kindly.

A Verse to Remember

DON'T GRUMBLE ABOUT
EACH OTHER.
JAMES 5:9

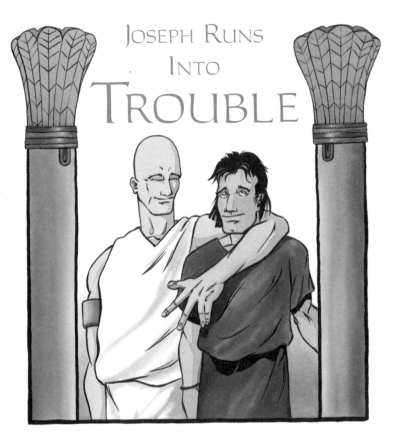

Joseph Runs Into Trouble

Joseph was far from home. He didn't know anyone, and he had to learn a new language. Worst of all, he was a slave!

Joseph's boss was a man named Potiphar. Joseph didn't want to be a slave, but he worked very hard, and God helped him. Soon Potiphar put him in charge of his whole house.

Then one day, Mrs. Potiphar told a terrible lie. "Joseph has been very bad to me," she said to Potiphar. "I want you to get rid of him."

Potiphar was very angry with Joseph. "I'm going to throw you in jail!" he said.

"I can't believe it!" Joseph said to himself. "I didn't do anything wrong."

Joseph worked hard in the jail. He didn't cause any trouble, and God helped him there, too. Soon he was in charge of all the other prisoners!

In jail Joseph was kind to a man who had once worked for the king. But when that man went back to work, he forgot all about Joseph.

Two years later, the king had some bad dreams. "Who can help me understand them?" he asked.

Then the king's assistant remembered that Joseph had once helped him understand a dream. "Joseph can help you," he told the king. So the king let Joseph out of jail. With God's help Joseph explained the dreams.

"You are very wise," said the king. "I want you to help me rule the country!" Joseph became the second most important man in all the land. And God continued to help him.

Based on Genesis 39-41

Making a Man of God

A MAN OF GOD REFUSES TO GIVE UP,
EVEN WHEN BAD THINGS HAPPEN.

Lots of bad things happened to Joseph, and none of them were his fault. His brothers sold him into slavery, his boss's wife lied about him, he was put in jail unfairly, and someone he helped forgot about him. But Joseph kept trusting God, and God helped him do the right things.

Do bad things ever happen to you? Is anyone ever mean to you? Have you ever been in trouble even though you didn't do anything wrong? Do you ever feel like giving up? Remember that God is with you. He will help you just like he helped Joseph!

Coaching Tips

Tell your young man about a time when things got so bad that you were tempted to give up doing right. What happened? What made you keep on the right track?

Explain that God is faithful. If we ask him, he will help us to do the right thing, no matter what. And he never gives up on us just because we sometimes fail.

A Verse to Remember

DON'T GET TIRED OF
DOING WHAT IS GOOD.
GALATIANS 6:9

A Surprise
REUNION

Jacob's family was running out of food. "There is plenty of food in Egypt," Jacob said to his sons. "Go buy some before we starve to death!"

When they arrived in Egypt, the brothers went to see the governor. "We want to buy food," they said.

They didn't know that the governor was their brother Joseph. They thought he was dead. But he had become a very powerful man in Egypt.

Joseph recognized his brothers, and he knew they had one more brother at home. Before he would sell them food, he said, "I will keep one of you here until you bring me your little brother."

The brothers were afraid. "We're being punished because of what we did to Joseph," they said to each other.

When they got home, they told their father what the governor had said.

"I've already lost one son," said Jacob. "I don't want to lose another."

But when the food ran out, the brothers had to
return to Egypt. At last Jacob let them take
their youngest brother, Benjamin, along.

   When they saw Joseph again, he invited them
to a big dinner. He gave Benjamin five times as
much food as anyone else!

The next day, Joseph couldn't wait any longer. "I am Joseph," he told them, "the brother you sold as a slave. You wanted to hurt me, but God turned it into something good." Then he hugged them all to show that he had forgiven them.

"Bring the rest of our family to Egypt," said Joseph. Now they could all be together again!

Based on Genesis 42-45

Making a Man of God

A MAN OF GOD FORGIVES OTHERS.

Joseph's brothers had been mean and cruel to him. They hated him so much they wanted him to die! But when Joseph had the chance to pay them back, he was kind to them instead. He chose forgiveness rather than getting even.

Has anyone ever done something mean to you? Did you want to hurt that person back? What do you think might have happened if you had said "I forgive you" instead?

Jesus forgives you when you ask. Now you can forgive others!

Coaching Tips

Few things are more difficult than offering genuine forgiveness to someone who has done you harm. But few lessons are more critical. Share some "forgiveness stories" from your own life—some that you got right, and some you wish you had done differently.

Explain the difference between a careless "don't worry about it" and a heartfelt "I forgive you." There is nothing casual about genuine forgiveness.

Remember that Jesus forgave his tormentors, even while hanging on the cross!

A Verse to Remember

BE KIND TO EACH OTHER . . .
FORGIVING ONE ANOTHER.
EPHESIANS 4:32

BASKET-BOAT

The King of Egypt had turned God's people into slaves, but he was afraid that there were too many of them. So he came up with a horrible plan to get rid of all the baby boys!

78

When Moses was born, his mother thought he was
beautiful. But she was afraid of the king, so she
kept him hidden for three months. It was pretty
hard to hide a noisy baby at home. So she hid
him in a waterproof basket and set it in the
water at the edge of the river.

"Watch your brother," she told Moses' sister.
"Make sure nothing bad happens to him."

One day, an Egyptian princess came to the river to take a bath. It wasn't long before she discovered the little basket-boat. And when her servant brought it to her, she opened it up and found little Moses inside. He began to cry and the princess felt sorry for him. She wanted to keep him.

Moses' sister was watching, and she had an idea. "Would you like me to find a woman to take care of the baby for you?" she asked.

"Oh, yes!" said the princess. "I will pay her to help me."

The princess didn't know that the woman was Moses'
mother. She paid her to take care of her own baby!
And Moses' family didn't have to hide him any more.

When Moses was a little older, he went to live
with the princess, and she treated him like her very
own son.

Based on Exodus 2

Making a Man of God

A MAN OF GOD IS PROTECTED.

Babies can't take care of themselves, can they? And Moses was no different than the babies you know. He was completely helpless. But God had a plan for Moses, and he wouldn't let anyone hurt him.

Can you take care of yourself? You can do a lot of things can't you? But even grownups need someone to protect them sometimes.

God wants to be your protector. You can ask him anytime.

Coaching Tips

Explain that having God's protection doesn't mean that nothing bad will ever happen to you. Even Moses had some bad experiences. But it does mean that God is looking out for you. Nothing can happen that he does not allow. And you can rely on God to help you through any circumstance, no matter how difficult or dangerous.

A Verse to Remember

THE LORD HIMSELF WATCHES OVER YOU.
PSALM 121:5

A Fiery Job Offer

Moses was way out in the country, taking care of some sheep, when he saw the strangest thing he had ever seen.

"Wow!" said Moses. "There's a bush on fire, but it isn't burning up. I've got to check this out."

When he got closer, he heard something. "Moses!" a voice called. "Moses!"

"I'm right here," he answered.

"Don't come any closer," said the voice. "It's me, God. And this is a holy place."

God? Moses was terrified, and he hid  his face in his hands.

"I have a job for you," said God. "The king of Egypt is treating your people very badly, so I have decided to rescue them. "I want you to be their leader."

"Who, me?" asked Moses. "How do you expect me to do that?"

"I will be with you," said God.

"But I don't think anyone will listen to me." Moses was starting to sweat. "Besides, I'm not a very good speaker. I never know the right words to say."

"I'll help you," said God, "And I'll tell you what to say."

"Please!" Moses begged. "Send someone else."

"Okay," said God, but he was getting a little upset with Moses. "Take your brother Aaron with you. He's a good speaker, and he will say what you tell him."

Finally, Moses agreed. He and Aaron called a meeting of their people and told them what God had said. When the people realized that God was going to rescue them, they bowed their heads and praised him.

Based on Exodus 3 & 4

Making a Man of God

A MAN OF GOD DEPENDS ON GOD, NOT ON HIS OWN ABILITY.

Moses didn't think he would make a very good leader, and maybe he was right. He wasn't very brave, he didn't speak very well, and he liked to make excuses. But with God helping him, Moses became one of the greatest leaders of all time!

Are you afraid to try something because you think you're not good enough? Is it something you think God wants you to do? Do you ever make excuses when you don't want to do something?

Pray and ask God to help you. With his help you can do great things!

Coaching Tips

Can you think of a time when your lack of courage or ability was overcome by God's help? Share an example from your own life or the life of someone you know.

Help your young man understand that whether he has great self-confidence or none at all, God is there to help him. Only God's ability is truly reliable.

A Verse to Remember

I CAN DO EVERYTHING WITH THE HELP OF CHRIST WHO GIVES ME THE STRENGTH I NEED.

PHILIPPIANS 4:13

GOD
GETS
PHARAOH'S
ATTENTION

God's people were slaves, and the king of Egypt was very cruel to them. So one day, Moses went to see the king.

"Let God's people go," he said.

"No way!" said the king. "I'm going to make them work even harder!"

Moses was discouraged. "It's worse than ever, God. Why did you send me to talk to him?"

"Pharaoh is very stubborn," said God. "But when he sees how powerful I am, he will let you go."

Then God sent disasters to Egypt: blood in the rivers, millions of frogs, swarms of insects, a terrible hail storm, sickness-even death. Before each disaster, Moses warned the king that something bad was about to happen. But the king was stubborn. Sometimes he promised to let the people go, but he always changed his mind.

Finally, the king gave in. So Moses called all the people together and they left. But by the time they got to the seashore, the king changed his mind again! This time he sent his soldiers to bring the people back.

With the sea in front of them and the soldiers behind them, the people had nowhere to run. They were scared.

"Hold your walking stick out over the sea," God told Moses.

So Moses held out his stick and God made a dry path through the water. All the people walked over to the other side. When the soldiers tried to follow, the water came crashing down on top of them.

God rescued his people, just as he had promised!

Based on Exodus 5-14

Making a Man of God

A MAN OF GOD BELIEVES
IN GOD'S POWER.

God did some amazing things in Egypt, things like turning a stick into a snake. But the king thought it was only a trick. He was too stubborn to believe in God's power. And because he didn't believe, his country was nearly ruined.

You are probably very strong. Are you as strong as a grown-up? Are grown-ups as strong as God? Can you think of some things God does that no one else can do?

Tell God you are glad he is so powerful.

Coaching Tips

Ever notice how easy it is to give nature, technology, or coincidence the credit for acts of God? Help your young man to discern God's powerful hand in the events of life. Tell him about a time when you saw God's power in a situation.

A Verse to Remember

O LORD MY GOD, HOW
GREAT YOU ARE!
PSALM 104:1

Food from
Heaven

After their amazing escape from Egypt, God's people began to travel through the desert.

It was hot and dry, and before long the people were very hungry.

"We wish we were back in Egypt," some people grumbled. "At least we had plenty to eat there."

"Yes," others agreed, "we're going to starve here in this desert."

Moses didn't know what to do. He knew they couldn't go back to Egypt. But there were no farms in the desert, and there were no stores where they could buy food. He decided to talk to God about the problem.

"I have heard the people complaining," said God. "Tell them that I will give them meat in the evening and bread in the morning. That way everyone will know that I am God."

So Moses called all the people together and told them what God was going to do. That very evening, a whole bunch of quail flew into the camp where the people were staying. The quail were easy to catch and they were very good to eat! Everyone had enough to eat that night.

The next morning, when the people woke up, the ground was covered with thin, white flakes.

"What is this stuff?" they asked Moses.

"It is the food God promised to give you," he replied.

"Mmmm. It tastes like honey cakes," they said. They called it manna, and each family gathered up as much they needed.

God kept sending manna and quail, and there was always plenty.

Based on Exodus 16

Making a Man of God

A MAN OF GOD KNOWS THAT GOD
WILL GIVE HIM WHAT HE NEEDS.

Even after all the amazing things God did
to help his people get out of Egypt, they
were still worried that he wouldn't take
care of them. It must have made God sad
to hear the people complaining instead of
trusting him.

God has done lots of amazing things for
people. Can you think of some others
besides the manna and quail in this story?
Instead of complaining, God wants us to
talk to him when we need something, just
like Moses did.

Coaching Tips

Our heavenly Father is even more concerned about our needs than our human parents. Often, however, he uses our parents (and others) to meet our needs. Look for an opportunity to personally demonstrate this by meeting some specific need. Help your young man to begin to see the hand of God behind the kindness of others.

Explain the difference between wants and needs.

A Verse to Remember

TELL GOD WHAT YOU NEED AND
THANK HIM FOR ALL
HE HAS DONE.
PHILIPPIANS 4:6

GOD'S
RULES

hile God's people were camping in the desert, Moses climbed up on a mountain to meet with God. He must have been scared. He couldn't see God because there were thick dark clouds of smoke all around him. The whole mountain shook and lightning was coming out of it. And God's voice sounded like thunder.

"I have some things I want you to tell my people," said God. "If they will obey the rules I give them, then I will take special care of them."

"The people say they will obey you," said Moses. "What do you want them to do?"

"Take two blocks of stone," said God, "and carve ten rules on them:"

These are the rules God gave Moses:

1. Don't worship other gods.
2. Don't make any idols.
3. Don't use God's name in a bad way.
4. Keep one day a week for rest and worship.
5. Treat your parents with honor.

So Moses carved the ten rules into the stones, just
as God told him to. Then he carried the stones down
the mountain to show all the people. Now everyone
would know for sure what God wanted them to do.

Based on Exodus 19-20

Making a Man of God

A MAN OF GOD
OBEYS GOD'S RULES.

People don't always like to follow God's rules. Sometimes we don't like anyone telling us what to do, do we? But God knows what is best for us. When we don't follow his rules, we may get hurt, or we may hurt someone else.

Can you think of some rules you don't like? What happens when you break the rules? Why do we have rules, anyway? Whose rules are the most important?

Coaching Tips

Take your young man for a drive. Ask him to guess what would happen if drivers ignored traffic lights, stop signs, lane markers, etc. Help him to see the connection between traffic rules and God's rules. Set a good example in both arenas.

Be sure he understands that God's love cannot be earned by keeping rules. Nothing he can do will make God love him more-or less!

A Verse to Remember

I WILL OBEY YOUR WONDERFUL LAWS.
PSALM 119:106

JETHRO'S GOOD
ADVICE

Moses was the leader of God's people and he was very busy. He told them what God wanted them to do. He taught them God's rules. When anyone had a problem, Moses decided what to do about it. If people had an argument, Moses helped them work it out.

When Jethro came to visit, he was surprised to see people standing in a long line just to talk to Moses.

"Why are you doing this all by yourself?" Jethro asked. "People have been waiting all day for you to help them."

"Well," said Moses, "I have to tell them what God wants. I have to teach them his rules. I have to settle their arguments."

"But this isn't a good way to do it," said Jethro.
"You will wear yourself out if you do it all by
yourself. And you will wear the people out, too."
Moses wondered if Jethro had a different idea.

"Why not find some smart, honest men to help you?" said Jethro. "They can be like judges over smaller groups of people. If a problem is too hard for them, or too important, they will let you decide. But most problems are small. Your helpers can take care of those."

Moses listened to Jethro, and he liked his idea. So he found some good men to help him. Jethro was right; the people had someone to listen to their problems without waiting all day. And Moses didn't have to work quite so hard.

Based on Exodus 18

Making a Man of God

A MAN OF GOD LISTENS TO GOOD ADVICE.

Moses was so busy doing things to help people that he was wearing himself out. And the people had to wait so long for help that they were getting worn out, too. Moses didn't know a better way to work. But Jethro did. He was a wise man. It was a good thing Moses listened to him.

Do your parents or your teachers ever tell you a better way to do something? Do you take their advice, or do you keep doing things your way. Why?

Coaching Tips

Offer some examples of people who rely on the wisdom of others (e.g., the President has a Cabinet, ministers have elders, deacons, etc., sports stars have coaches and trainers). The most successful people are often those getting the best advice. Advice that comes from God is the best advice of all.

Who do you go to for advice? A pastor, a friend, a family member, a mentor? Tell your young man. Then, let him know that he can come to you for advice any time.

A Verse to Remember

THOSE WHO TAKE ADVICE ARE WISE.
PROVERBS 13:10

GOD'S
EXPLORERS

God promised to give the land across the river
to his people so they would have their very
own country. He told Moses to send some men to
explore the land so that the people would know
just how good it was.

So Moses chose twelve men and sent them to check out the land. "Go see what it is like," he told them. "Then come back and tell us about it."

So Joshua, Caleb, and ten other men went exploring. They learned about the farms and the cities, as well as the people who lived there.

They even brought back some fruit that grew in the new land. One bunch of grapes was so big that it took two men to carry it between them!

"It is true that there is food everywhere," said the men when they returned from exploring. "We even brought you some. But the people there have big forts and they are a lot stronger than we are. Some of them are giants. We felt like grasshoppers next to them!"

But Caleb and Joshua disagreed. "This land is wonderful," they said. "And the Lord can keep us safe and give us the land. Don't be afraid of the people there. They are helpless, because God is with us."

But God's people were too afraid. They wouldn't listen to Joshua and Caleb. So God decided that everyone who was afraid would not get to see the new land. Only Joshua and Caleb got to live there.

Based on Numbers 13 & 14

Making a Man of God

A MAN OF GOD IS BOLD.

What made Joshua and Caleb bold when the other ten explorers were afraid? The ten men saw the giants, and they looked big compared to them. Joshua and Caleb saw the giants, too, but they knew that those giants were small compared to God. Do you see the difference?

Are you ever afraid because a problem looks too big for you? How big is God? Is he bigger than your problem? Do you think he will help you?

Coaching Tips

Optimism often comes from a positive outlook on circumstances. It can crumble when circumstances look bad. But boldness comes from knowing that God is with you, and that he is able to overcome any circumstances. Can your young man see the difference between optimism and boldness by watching how you respond to circumstances in your life?

A Verse to Remember

THE LORD YOUR GOD IS WITH YOU
WHEREVER YOU GO.
JOSHUA 1:9

MOSES'
BIG MISTAKE

Moses was leading God's people to the land God had promised them. It was a very long trip, and the people were hot and tired. Sometimes they had to camp in the desert. They complained a lot.

One day they camped in a place where there was no water to drink. The people got very upset and started blaming Moses.

"Did you bring us here to die?" they said. "Why did you make us leave Egypt? This is a terrible place. There isn't even any water to drink!"

Moses didn't know what to do, so he began to pray.

"Gather everyone together," God told him. "Then order that rock over there to start spouting water. You will get enough water for everyone."

So Moses called God's people together. But he was tired of their complaining, and he didn't like being blamed for their problems. He became very angry.

"Listen, you troublemakers!" he shouted. "Do I have to get water out of a rock?"

Then he took his walking stick and hit the rock.
  Nothing happened.
  He was really mad now, so he hit the rock
again. This time, water came out in a rush.
There was so much water that everyone had
enough to drink. Even the animals had plenty.

But God was saddened by what Moses did. Moses was supposed to speak to the rock, but instead, he got angry and hit it.

"You may not take my people into the new land I am giving them," God said.

Based on Numbers 20

Making a Man of God

A MAN OF GOD CONTROLS HIS ANGER.

Moses loved God, and he wanted to help God's people. He wasn't a bad man. But when he got angry, he disobeyed God. He was too mad to listen to what God said. If he had listened and obeyed, God wouldn't have punished him.

Do you ever get angry? What makes you angry? Are you a good listener when you are angry?

Ask God to help you listen and obey.

Coaching Tips

Reassure your young man that everyone gets angry. Anger is a natural emotion. But anger does not need to be expressed through aggressive behavior. That only results in doing harm to ourselves and others.

How do you handle your anger? Do you think and pray before acting out your anger in harmful ways? Can a young man follow your example with confidence?

A Verse to Remember

PEOPLE WITH GOOD SENSE RESTRAIN THEIR ANGER.

PROVERBS 19:11

A Voice
in the
Night

Samuel was not very old, but he had a very important job. He was a helper for Eli, the priest in God's temple. Eli was getting very old and he was almost blind.

One night, after Eli went to bed, Samuel heard a voice.

"Samuel! Samuel!" the voice called. Samuel jumped out of bed and ran into Eli's room. "Here I am," he said. "What do you need?"

"I didn't call you," said Eli. "Go back to bed."

So Samuel went back to his room and lay down.

"Samuel!" It was the voice again.

Samuel went to Eli's room again. "Here I am," he said. "What do you need?"

Eli looked puzzled. "I didn't call you," he said.

The voice called a third time and Samuel went straight to Eli's room. "Here I am," he said. "What do you need?"

"God must be calling you," Eli said, "The next time you hear the voice, say, 'Yes, Lord, your servant is listening.'"

When Samuel heard the voice again, he answered just as Eli had said. And God gave him a message. But it wasn't very good news.

"What did God tell you?" Eli asked when Samuel got up the next morning. Samuel was afraid to tell Eli, but he knew he had to.

"Your family is in trouble," he said, "because you have all disobeyed God."

Eli looked sad, but he knew God was right.

After that, God spoke often to Samuel and all the people listened to him.

Based on 1 Samuel 3

Making a Man of God

A MAN OF GOD LISTENS TO WHAT GOD SAYS.

When Samuel heard God's words, he paid attention. God doesn't normally talk to us out loud, but we need to pay attention to what he says, too. His message to us is in the Bible.

Can you read the Bible for yourself? Can you listen while someone else reads? Either way, you can learn what God wants to tell you.

All the stories in this book come from the Bible. Can you remember any of them? Which one is your favorite?

Coaching Tips

Take a few moments to show your young man your own Bible. Why is it important to you? Explain what God wants you to learn from it.

This may be a good time to give the young man his own Bible, if he doesn't already own one.

A Verse to Remember

THE WORD OF GOD IS FULL OF LIVING POWER.
HEBREWS 4:12

Big
Enough

"**C**hoose your best man and let him fight me,"
Goliath shouted to the army of God's people. But
the soldiers were scared. Goliath was huge—over nine
feet tall! How could anyone fight a man
that big?

When
David came
to the army
camp to
visit his big
brothers,
he could
hardly
believe his
eyes.

"Who does this Goliath think he is?" he asked. "Why do you let him insult God's people?"

"Go home and take care of your sheep," growled his brother.

But David went to see the king. "I'll fight the giant," he said.

"Don't be silly. You are just a boy!" said the king.

"The Lord helped me when wild animals attacked my sheep," David replied. "I know he will help me now, too."

Finally, the king agreed. "May the Lord be with you."

So David took his sling, and his shepherd's stick, and five smooth rocks.

When Goliath saw him coming he roared, "Why did you bring a stick? Do you think I am a dog?" Then he made fun of David and used lots of bad words.

"I come in the name of the Lord," shouted David, "and he doesn't need big weapons like yours!"

David put one of the smooth rocks in his sling, whirled it around and around and around and let it fly. The rock hit Goliath on the head. The giant stumbled and fell flat on his face! The fight was over.

Goliath's soldiers were so scared they ran away.

Based on
1 Samuel 17

Making a Man of God

A MAN OF GOD IS BRAVE.

Just like the soldiers, David could see that Goliath was a giant, and that his weapons were dangerous. But he knew that God is more powerful than any giant. And even though he was too young to be a soldier, David knew that God would help him.

Do you ever think that you are too small or too young to do anything important? God will help you, no matter how old you are or how big you are. And if God is helping you, doesn't that make you feel brave?

Coaching Tips

Let your young man know that you value the size of his heart much more than the size of his body—and so does God.

Being brave isn't about being big, strong, or smart. It's about having faith that God will take care of you, no matter what.

A Verse to Remember

Be strong with the Lord's mighty power.

Ephesians 6:10

BEST FRIENDS

Everywhere David went, people said how great he was. He was the most popular man in the country. That made King Saul very jealous. Sometimes he got so angry that David had to hide from him.

Jonathan, the king's son, wasn't jealous at all. David was his best friend and Jonathan didn't want anything bad to happen to him. Together they made a plan to help David escape if the king became too angry.

"Why didn't David join us for dinner?" the king asked one night. When Jonathan tried to answer, the king flew into a rage. "Go and get him so I can kill him!" he shouted.

Jonathan was ashamed of his father and he knew he would have to warn his friend. David was in more trouble than ever!

Jonathan went out into the field where he knew David was hiding and shot his bow and arrows.

"Hurry," he told the boy who came to gather his
arrows. "One arrow is still ahead of you." That was
the signal he and David had agreed on. It meant
David would have to hide far away.

As soon as the boy went back into the city, David
came out of his hiding place. He and Jonathan
hugged each other. They were sad to think that they
might never see each other again.

"We have promised to be friends forever," said
Jonathan when it was time to go, "and we will trust
the Lord."

Based on 1 Samuel 20

Making a Man of God

A MAN OF GOD IS A FAITHFUL FRIEND.

Jonathan was a true friend. He helped David even when he knew it would make the king angry. He knew that what King Saul wanted to do was wrong. And he wasn't embarrassed to show how much David meant to him.

Who is your best friend? How do you show your friendship to others? Would you stand up for your friend if he were in trouble?

Coaching Tips

Who was your best friend when you were growing up? Tell your young man about him and why his friendship was important to you. Talk about your current friends and what they mean to you as well.

Begin building a lifelong friendship with your son by discovering—and pursuing—what is important to him. Let him know you will always stand up for him.

Explain to your young man how Jonathan's love for David models Jesus' love for us.

A Verse to Remember

A FRIEND IS ALWAYS LOYAL.
PROVERBS 17:17

FIRE AND WATER

Elijah, the man of God, was angry with God's people.

"You won't obey God's rules," he told them, "and you are worshiping other gods. You have to decide: if God is real, you must follow him. But if some other god is real, then follow him."

The people didn't say a word.

So Elijah suggested a contest. "I will make an offering to God, and your leaders can make an offering to another god," he said. "Then we will pray for fire to burn up the offerings. The one who sends fire will be the true God."

The other leaders thought this was a good idea.

"You go first," said Elijah.

So the leaders made an offering and began to pray. But no fire started. They prayed all morning. They even shouted to their god and danced all around. Still no fire.

"Shout louder," Elijah teased. "Your god is probably busy, or maybe he took a trip. Is he asleep? Wake him up!"

The leaders kept shouting and doing crazy things all afternoon. But there was no fire. Nothing happened at all.

Finally, Elijah made his offering to God. Then he poured water all over it until it was completely soaked.

All of a sudden, fire came down from the sky and burned up the offering. But it didn't stop there. It burned up the rocks, the dirt, and even the water!

Now everyone knew for sure who the one true God was.

Based on
1 Kings 19

Making a Man of God

A MAN OF GOD WORSHIPS THE ONE TRUE GOD.

Just like the people in Elijah's story, some people today don't want to follow God's rules. They act as if some things are more important than God, and they forget how powerful he is. Or maybe they don't understand how much God loves them.

Think of two or three of your very favorite things. Are they more important than God? Perhaps you can pray and tell God how important he is to you.

Coaching Tips

Consider the material blessings or desires that sometimes threaten to become top priority in your life. Using these as examples, point out how easy it is to "worship other gods."

Start a discussion by asking, "What is God like?" Focus on his uniqueness.

A Verse to Remember

FOR THERE IS ONLY ONE GOD.
1 TIMOTHY 2:5

THE OIL BUSINESS

The two brothers were worried. Their dad had died and Mom was raising them all by herself. But she didn't have a job, and they had no food. They didn't know what to do. Now someone was trying to take the boys away from their mom.

So they went to see their friend, Elisha. He was a man of God, and God often told him what to do to help people.

"What do you have in your house?" he asked.

"Nothing except a bottle of olive oil," Mom said.

"Borrow empty jars from your friends and neighbors," said Elijah. "Get as many as you can."

So the two boys collected lots of empty jars. Then they watched as Mom took the bottle of olive oil and poured some into the first jar. When it was full, she poured some into the next jar, all the way to the top.

The bottle of oil wasn't very big. But Mom just kept pouring and pouring. And the boys kept bringing her jar after jar. They could hardly believe their eyes. Soon there were jars everywhere, and they were all filled with oil!

"Bring me another jar," Mom said.

But there weren't any more. And just then the bottle of oil ran dry.

When they told Elisha what had happened, he knew just what to do. "Sell all the olive oil," he said. "Then you can pay all your bills. There will be enough money left over to take care of your family."

Based on 2 Kings 4

Making a Man of God

A MAN OF GOD TRUSTS GOD,
EVEN IN HARD TIMES.

The boys in the story were having a hard time, weren't they? Their father was dead, their mom didn't have a job, and they didn't have any money to buy food. But God used Elisha to help them. Can you imagine how surprised they were when the oil kept pouring out of the bottle?

Has your family ever had any hard times? What happened?

Do you know anyone who is having a hard time right now? Pray and ask God to help them, too.

Coaching Tips

Tell about an experience you have had with hard times. Perhaps it involved a job loss, the loss of a loved one, some unexpected difficulty, or a big disappointment. How did God help you? Did he use another person to help, like he used Elisha in the story?

Are you experiencing a hard time right now? Let your young man know about it (at least in general terms) so he can watch how God will provide for you.

A Verse to Remember

My help comes from the Lord.
Psalm 121:2

THE MIRACLE
BATH

Naaman was
an important
man. He was the
leader of a very
large army, and
he had won
many battles.
But there was
something
wrong with
Naaman—he had
leprosy, a
horrible skin
disease.

Naaman's wife had a servant girl who believed in God. One day the girl said to Mrs. Naaman, "I wish Mr. Naaman would go to see Elisha, the man of God. Elisha can heal him."

That sounded like a good idea to Naaman. He really wanted to be healed. So he took some presents along and went with some of his officers to Elisha's house. He waited by the door until Elisha sent a messenger outside.

"Elisha says to go and wash yourself seven times in the Jordan River," said the messenger. "Then your skin will look like new. You will be healed."

Naaman got really mad and stomped away.
"Elisha didn't even come out to see me," he
complained. "I thought he would wave his
hands and call out to God! And what is wrong
with the rivers where I live? What's so special
about the Jordan River?"

"But sir," his officers said, "if Elisha had told you to do something hard, wouldn't you would have done it? Why not do this simple thing he told you?"

Finally, Naaman changed his mind and went to the Jordan River. He washed himself six times. On the seventh time, he looked down and saw that his skin was as healthy as a child's. He was healed!

Based on 2 Kings 5

Making a Man of God

A MAN OF GOD IS HUMBLE.

Naaman wanted to be healed from his disease. But even more, he wanted Elisha to treat him like a very important person. At first he was too proud to do what Elisha told him, and he almost went home. What would have happened if he hadn't washed in the river?

Do you ever get upset when people don't do what you want? Do you sometimes think you are more important than others?

How can you show others that they are important, too?

Coaching Tips

Remind your young man that he is very important—to you, and to God. But, of course, everyone is important to God, even those who don't seem important at all. That should make everyone important to us, too. And when we treat others as if they are important, we won't worry so much about how important we are.

Does your young man know who is important when he is with you?

A Verse to Remember

BE HUMBLE, THINKING OF OTHERS AS BETTER THAN YOURSELF.
PHILIPPIANS 2:3

THE YOUNGEST KING

Josiah was only eight years old when he became king! But even though he was very young, he wanted to be a good king. He loved God and wanted to please him.

Many of God's people didn't worship in God's house anymore. They joined other religions and ignored God's rules. They stopped taking care of God's house.

"I want to make God's house beautiful again," said King Josiah. So he sent workers to clean it up and to repair anything that was broken. The workers did a good job, and soon God's house looked like new again.

While they were cleaning, the workers found something. "Look," they said. "We found a copy of God's Word!" They took it to King Josiah right away.

"Have someone read it to me," said the king. But when he heard what was written in God's Word he became very sad.

"We have not been doing what God's Word says we must do," he told the workers.

So King Josiah told his helpers to gather all the
people together. They stood in front of God's
house. Then the king read God's Word to them.

"I am going to keep God's rules with all my heart
from now on," he said when he was done reading,
"And I want you to do the same." All the people
agreed.

For the rest of King Josiah's life, he and his
people followed God and lived the way God's Word
told them to.

Based on 2 Chronicles 34

Making a Man of God

A MAN OF GOD WANTS TO
BE CLOSE TO GOD.

King Josiah's people didn't care very much about God's house. They didn't come to worship anymore. And they didn't obey God's Word, either. They didn't care about God at all.

But Josiah did. He wanted to be close to God. He wanted God to bless him.

Can you think of ways to show God you want to be close to him? He wants to be close to you!

Coaching Tips

Your attitude toward worship says a lot about what you think of God, and so does you view of the Bible. Are you keeping your distance? Or can your desire for closeness to God be seen in your worship and study habits? Chances are, your young man will come to care about what you care about.

Make sure that he has the opportunity to worship on a regular basis. See that he gets his very own Bible. Then read it with him whenever you can.

A Verse to Remember

DRAW CLOSE TO GOD, AND GOD WILL DRAW CLOSE TO YOU.
JAMES 4:8

A JOB TO DO

"What's the matter, Nehemiah?" the king asked his helper. "You look sad. Are you sick?"

"I'm sad because the city where I grew up is ruined," said Nehemiah.

"What can I do to help?" asked the king.

Nehemiah said a quick prayer. Then he told the king, "I want to go back home and fix up my city."

So the king sent Nehemiah on his way.

When Nehemiah arrived in his city he saw what a mess it was. Walls were broken down. The gates had been burned. There was trash everywhere.

Nehemiah called the people together. "Let's fix up our city so we can be proud of it again," he told them.

"Good idea!" the people said. "Let's get to work!"

So Nehemiah organized all the people who wanted to help him. Each person had a job to do, and they worked together.

Some people didn't like what Nehemiah was doing. They began to make fun of him. But Nehemiah just prayed and kept working.

Then some people planned to come and wreck
Nehemiah's work. Nehemiah prayed and put guards
around the city.

"We're getting tired," some of the workers
grumbled. "There is too much work to do." Nehemiah
reminded them that God would help them.

Nehemiah worked hard, and the people followed his example. And with God's help, they finished the job in record time!

"It's time to celebrate!" Nehemiah told the people. "This is a special day!"

His plan had worked. He was proud of his city once more.

Based on Nehemiah 1-8

Making a Man of God

A MAN OF GOD IS A LEADER.

Nehemiah didn't wait for anyone else to take care of his city. He decided to do something about it himself. That is what made him a leader.

Can you become a leader? You can if you can clean your room without being asked. Maybe you can pick up litter in the playground. Or collect some clothes for needy children. Do you have any other ideas?

Coaching Tips

Leading is hard work. Without God's help it is even harder. Notice how Nehemiah prayed about everything. Remember to model the importance of prayer.

Every leader runs into obstacles: criticism, opposition, complaining, etc. Encourage your young man to keep going, even when the going is tough!

A Verse to Remember

Be an example.
Titus 2:7

ESTHER'S
DANGEROUS
MISSION

The king of Persia was very rich. He ruled a big kingdom that stretched from Africa all the way to India. But in spite of all that, he wasn't very happy. He didn't like his queen anymore, he wanted a new queen.

So he decided to hold a contest. Beautiful
women came to the palace from all over the
kingdom. Esther, a young Jewish woman was
one of those who came. Everyone was very
impressed with her. When she went to see the
king, he loved her more than all the others.
That's how Esther became queen.

Now Haman, one of the king's trusted helpers, hated God's people, the Jews, and planned to kill them all. When Esther heard about it, she was very scared. She needed to talk to the king about this horrible plan. But the king was very strict. No one was allowed to come and see him without an invitation–not even the queen! So Esther asked God's people to pray for her.

"I'm going to see the king," she said. "I am willing to die if I have to." If she didn't talk to the king, a lot of other people would die.

When the king saw Esther, he was glad she had come. He offered to give her whatever she wanted. So she told him about Haman and the awful plan to kill God's people.

The king was so angry that he got rid of Haman. But for Esther, the best part was that God's people were saved.

Based on Esther 1-10

Making a Man of God

A MAN OF GOD SHOWS COURAGE.

Esther was afraid, so she prayed that God would help her. Then she did the right thing. That's what courage is: doing the right thing even when you are afraid.

Do you ever get scared? Everyone does sometimes. What makes you scared? What do you do about it? The next time it happens, try doing what Esther did. God will give you the courage you need.

Coaching Tips

Think of some people you know who demonstrate unusual courage and tell their stories.

Are there ways in which your young man already shows courage? Commend him and encourage him to thank God for it.

Emphasize the fact that courage isn't the absence of fear, but doing right in spite of fear. If we aren't afraid, no courage is necessary!

A Verse to Remember

WHEN I AM AFRAID, I PUT MY
TRUST IN YOU.
PSALM 56:3

PROBLEMS
AND MORE
PROBLEMS

Job was a good man who obeyed God. He loved his wife and ten children very much. He owned thousands of animals and he had many workers. In fact, Job was the richest man around. And he thanked God for everything.

One day a man brought a message to Job: "Your enemies stole your cattle and donkeys and killed your workers!"

Then another messenger arrived: "Your sheep and your shepherds all died in a big fire!"

A third messenger said, "Bad men stole your camels and killed your workers!"

Job didn't know what to say. And before he could think of anything, another messenger ran up.

"Your children were having a party at your oldest son's house," he said. "All of a sudden, a storm blew the house down, and killed them all!"

Job was terribly sad. First his animals were gone,
then his workers—and now all of his children.
Could anything else go wrong?

Before long, Job got very sick. He had
horrible sores all over his body, and he felt
awful. His wife thought he should just give up
and die! And his friends said discouraging
things, too.

But Job didn't stop loving God, even though he felt sick and sad. "The Lord gave me everything I had," he said, "and the Lord has taken it away. Praise the name of the Lord!"

When Job got better, God blessed him with ten more children. And God made him twice as rich as he was before.

Based on Job 1, 2, and 42

Making a Man of God

A MAN OF GOD LOVES GOD NO
MATTER WHAT.

Some people thought Job loved God just because he was rich. Maybe they thought he really only liked the things God gave him. But even when he was poor and sick, Job still loved God just as much.

What was more important to Job, his stuff or God? How can you tell?

What do you think about God when you are sick? When you are sad? When you don't have all the things you want?

Coaching Tips

How do you measure up when the tests of life come along? Can your young man see that your faith is not dependent on circumstances?

This is a great time to remember that God loves us—no matter what. He knows exactly what we are like, yet he still sent Jesus to die for us (Romans 5:8).

A Verse to Remember

I WILL PRAISE THE LORD AT ALL TIMES.
PSALM 34:1

DANIEL'S DANGEROUS
PRAYER

Daniel worked for a king in a faraway place. He was the king's very best helper.

Every day when he went home, Daniel got down on his knees and asked God to help him.

Some of the kings other helpers were always
trying to get him in trouble. But Daniel worked
very hard and got along well with the king.

One day Daniel heard about a new law:
Everyone must pray only to the king or they
would be fed to wild lions.

Daniel went right home and got down on his knees, just like he always did. "Please help me, God," he prayed. "I will only worship you."

Soon, soldiers came and arrested him. "You were praying to God and not to the king," they said. "Someone saw you through your window."

Daniel knew he was in big trouble. The soldiers took
him to the place where the wild lions were kept. They
threw him inside and put a huge stone over the
door. It was dark inside, and there was no way for
Daniel to get away.

The king was very upset. He liked Daniel and he didn't want to hurt him, but he had been tricked into making a bad law. He was so worried that he didn't sleep all night. The next morning, the king went to see if Daniel was still alive.

"Did your God save you?" he shouted.

"Yes," answered Daniel. "God sent an angel to shut the lions' mouths."

Daniel wasn't even scratched.

Based on Daniel 6

Making a Man of God

A MAN OF GOD ISN'T AFRAID TO WORSHIP GOD.

Daniel knew it was silly to pray to the king; the king was just a man. He prayed to God because he knew God is powerful. Only God could answer his prayers and save him from the lions. Besides, he knew that God's rules are more important than the rules people make.

God wants everyone to pray to him. What would you do if someone told you not to? What would you do if other kids saw you praying and began making fun of you?

Coaching Tips

Daniel faced severe persecution. But persecution is not something that only happened to people in Bible times. Tell about a time when you (or someone you know) was mistreated because of your faith. Was it hard?

Explain that while most of us are free to pray and go to church, there are places in our world today where people face fines, imprisonment, and worse, all because they choose to worship God.

A Verse to Remember

I WILL PRAISE THE LORD
AS LONG AS I LIVE.
PSALM 146:2

THE GIANT FISH

"Go to the great city of Nineveh," God said to Jonah. God had a message for the people there.

But Jonah didn't want to go to Nineveh. He knew that the people there were very cruel and he didn't think they would like God's message. So he got on a ship that was sailing in the other direction.

If I go far away, maybe God won't find me, he thought. And Jonah lay down in the ship's hold and went to sleep.

But God sent a storm and soon the little ship was in trouble. It was almost ready to sink! The sailors did everything they could to save their ship, but they were scared. The captain went to find Jonah.

"How can you sleep at a time like this?" he asked Jonah. "Get up and pray."

The sailors decided that the storm must be Jonah's fault. "Who are you?" they asked. "What have you done?"

Jonah admitted that he was running away from God. "This is all my fault," he told them. "Throw me into the sea."

When the sailors threw Jonah over the side, the storm stopped.

But Jonah was in deep water. God sent a giant fish along and before Jonah knew what was happening, the fish swallowed him! He was trapped!

After three days, Jonah prayed to God, and the fish spit him up on the beach. This time when God told him to go to Nineveh, Jonah went. And the people heard his message and worshiped God.

Based on Jonah 1-3

Making a Man of God

A MAN OF GOD OBEYS QUICKLY.

Jonah had a very dangerous adventure, didn't he? He should have gone to Nineveh as God asked in the first place. Instead, he did what he wanted to do and ended up in a lot of trouble.

When Mom or Dad or your teacher ask you to do something, do you always obey right away? Do you sometimes take your time? Obeying quickly is what God wants you to do. That will keep you out of trouble.

Coaching Tips

An important lesson from Jonah's story is that God sometimes gives us second chances. Tell about a time when you failed to obey right away. Did you pay a price for your willfulness? Were you given a second opportunity? How would things have turned out differently if you had obeyed quickly the first time?

Don't hesitate to give your young man a second chance when he fails.

A Verse to Remember

I PROMISE TO OBEY YOUR WORDS.
PSALM 119:57

No Room

Joseph was tired of traveling. He and Mary had been on the road to Bethlehem for more than seventy miles—but it seemed like forever! He knew that Mary was even more tired than he was because she was expecting a baby.

Finally Joseph saw the little village up ahead. "I'll try to find a room to rent so we can get some rest," he said.

"I hope you can find one soon," said Mary. "I don't think this baby will wait much longer."

"You mean—" Joseph was worried.

Mary smiled. "Yes, I think it's time for this special baby to be born."

Joseph hurried from place to place, looking for a room for the night. But the town was filled with travelers, and all of the rooms were already taken.

"I don't have any rooms left," said the man at the inn. "You'll have to try somewhere else."

"Please, sir," Joseph pleaded. "Mary is about to have a baby. I can't just let her sleep out on the street."

"Well," said the man, "I suppose you can sleep in the stable."

"With the animals?"

"Sorry, it's the best I can do."

So Joseph did the best he could to make Mary comfortable in the stable. And just as Mary had said, it wasn't long before her special baby was born. She wrapped him up snugly and laid him in the little bed Joseph made from the animals' feed trough.

They named the baby Jesus.

Based on Luke 2:1-7

Making a Man of God

A MAN OF GOD MAKES ROOM FOR JESUS.

What do you think the man at the inn would have said if he had known that Mary's baby was Jesus, the Son of God? Do you think he would have been more kind to Mary and Joseph? Would he have sent them to the stable? Maybe he would have let them stay in his room!

What would you do if Jesus wanted to stay at your house, or if he needed something you have? Would your answer be the same if you didn't know it was Jesus?

Coaching Tips

Explain what Jesus meant when he said, "When you did it to one of the least of these my brothers and sisters, you were doing it to me" (Matthew 25:40). Discuss a few ideas for "making room" for Jesus by showing kindness to others. Choose one idea and carry it out.

A Verse to Remember

IF WE LOVE EACH OTHER,
GOD LIVES IN US.
1 JOHN 4:12

TELLING THE
GOOD NEWS

The night Jesus was born, some shepherds were out in the fields around Bethlehem, taking care of their sheep and protecting them.

Suddenly, they saw a bright light shining all around them.

Then an angel of God seemed to come out of nowhere! The shepherds were scared to death!

"Don't be afraid," said the angel. "I've got some really great news that should make everyone happy!"

"Wh-wh-what news?" stammered one of the shepherds.

"The Savior-the one God promised to send-was just born in Bethlehem!"

"There are probably lots of babies in Bethlehem," said another shepherd. "How will we know which one is the Savior?"

"He's wrapped in strips of cloth," said the angel, "and lying in the animals' feed trough."

Before the other shepherds could say anything, a lot of other angels showed up and began praising God. After a while they all disappeared into heaven again.

"Come on," said the first shepherd. "Let's
go down to the village."

"Let's check it out," said another. "This is
wonderful news God has sent us!"

So they hurried into Bethlehem and
found Mary and Joseph in the stable. And
just as the angel said, the baby was lying in
the feed trough.

The shepherds were so excited that they talked about it to everyone they saw. "An angel told us that this baby is the Savior God promised," they said. And even after they went back to take care of their sheep they couldn't stop talking about it and praising God.

Based on Luke 2:8-20

Making a Man of God

A MAN OF GOD TELLS THE GOOD
NEWS ABOUT JESUS.

The shepherds were very excited about the good news. They knew something about the tiny baby in the stable that most people didn't. They knew he was God's Son, the Savior of the world! No wonder they wanted to tell everyone about him.

Has anyone ever told you the good news about Jesus? Can you tell someone else why Jesus is special? Who would you like to tell?

229

Coaching Tips

Make a point of reading the "Christmas story" throughout the year. By emphasizing the message of the angels—that Jesus is the Savior, the one God promised—you will help your young man to understand the purpose in Jesus' birth, not just the facts.

Encourage him by your example to talk openly about Jesus and the Good News.

A Verse to Remember

THE SAVIOR . . . HAS BEEN BORN TONIGHT IN BETHLEHEM.
LUKE 2:11

Satan's Tricks

Jesus was traveling by himself a long way from any towns. There were no stores or restaurants and he hadn't eaten any food for forty days. He was getting really hungry when Satan came to see him.

"If you are really God's Son," Satan said, "why don't you prove it by turning these rocks into bread?" Satan knew who Jesus was and he was trying to trick him.

But Jesus wouldn't do what Satan wanted. "God's Word says that people need more than just bread," he said. "They also need to pay attention to everything God says."

Then Satan took Jesus into the city, to the top of the temple. It was a long way down to the street below.

"If you are really God's Son," Satan said, "why don't you prove it by jumping off? God's Word says that the angels will protect you. You won't even stub your toe!"

"God's Word also says not to give God a test," answered Jesus. And he refused to jump.

Satan decided to try one more trick. He took Jesus up to the top of a very high mountain.

"Do you see all these countries?" he asked Jesus. "Aren't they great? Well, I will give them all to you. All you have to do is kneel down and worship me."

"Get out of here, Satan!" said Jesus. "God's
Word says that you must worship God, and
serve only him."

So Satan went away. His tricks hadn't worked.

After he was gone, angels came and took
care of Jesus.

Based on Matthew 4

Making a Man of God

A MAN OF GOD IS READY FOR SATAN'S TRICKS.

Satan had a lot of tricks, didn't he? But every time he tried to trick Jesus, Jesus remembered what God's Word says.

God's Word says that Satan is our enemy. He tries to get us to do bad things, even when we know we shouldn't. We call that temptation. Can you think of some ways he might try to tempt you? What should you do? Can you do what Jesus' did?

Coaching Tips

Tell your young man about a time when you were tempted to do something you knew was wrong. Did you remember to follow Jesus' example in this story? Being honest about a failure will give you a chance to explain that God's forgiveness is available when we confess and turn from the wrong we have done.

Help your young man remember (memorize) small portions of God's Word. Perhaps you can begin with the verse that follows.

A Verse to Remember

WHEN YOU ARE TEMPTED, [GOD] WILL SHOW YOU A WAY OUT SO THAT YOU WILL NOT GIVE IN TO IT.

1 CORINTHIANS 10:13

THROUGH THE ROOF

When people found out that Jesus was visiting their town, they told their friends. They had heard about the wonderful things Jesus did and they wanted to see for themselves. So they came to the house where he was staying.

Soon the house was full—there wasn't room
for even one more person. Some people
stood around outside, trying to hear what
Jesus was saying.

Four men arrived carrying their friend on
a mat between them. Their friend was
paralyzed—he couldn't walk, or even move his
arms and legs.

The men hoped Jesus could help him. But the house was so crowded they couldn't get close to Jesus.

"How are we going to help our friend if we can't get inside?" they wondered. They couldn't get in through the door. They couldn't get in through the windows. But they wouldn't give up. They loved their friend and he needed help.

"Let's try the roof!" they decided.

So they climbed up on the roof and carried their friend along. They began to make a hole in the roof. When the hole was big enough they lowered their paralyzed friend right down in front of Jesus!

When Jesus saw the man and how much faith his friends had, he said, "Your sins are forgiven. Stand up, take your mat, and go on home, because you are healed."

Suddenly, the man could move. His arms and legs felt strong again. He jumped up and hurried outside.

Everyone who saw it was amazed.

Based on Mark 2

Making a Man of God

A MAN OF GOD SHOWS HIS
FAITH BY DOING GOOD.

What if the four friends had said, "The house is too full," or "Jesus is too busy, let's not bother him?" What if they said, "We hope you get better," but they just stayed home? Do you think their friend would have been healed?

Jesus saw that the men had faith in him. How could he tell?

How can you show that you have faith in Jesus?

Coaching Tips

Explain that good deeds are not a substitute for faith. You cannot earn God's grace. Rather, doing good is evidence of your faith. The men in the story took their friend to Jesus because they believed Jesus could heal him. They acted on what they believed, and their friend was never the same!

Jesus said that the two greatest commandments were 1) Love God, and 2) Love others. There are many ways to show such love. True faith in Jesus, however, always results in more than just talk.

A Verse to Remember

I WILL SHOW YOU MY FAITH THROUGH MY GOOD DEEDS.
JAMES 2:18

THE MIRACLE
PICNIC

"Mother, may I go to see Jesus today?" asked a young boy.

"Yes," his mother replied, "but pack a lunch. I don't want you to go hungry."

"I'll take some bread and fish," said the boy. "That should be plenty for me."

When the boy arrived where Jesus was, a very large crowd had gathered. The boy got as close as he could so he wouldn't miss a single word the amazing teacher said. Soon he became so interested in Jesus that he forgot all about eating lunch.

When it started getting late, Jesus asked some of his friends, "Where can we buy bread to feed these people?"

"We don't have enough money to feed them all!" a man answered.

"Did anyone bring some food they can share?" asked Jesus.

"I did," said the boy, and he gave his food to one of Jesus' friends.

"What good will this do?" asked Jesus' friend. "There are more than five thousand people here, and this is only a little bread and a couple of dried fish."

Maybe he's right, thought the boy. My lunch is too small to make even a tiny snack for this crowd.

But Jesus just smiled and said, "Tell everyone to sit down." When everyone was seated on the grass, Jesus gave thanks and started passing out the food. Everyone had enough to eat and there was lots of food left over—all from one small lunch!

"Wow!" said the boy. "Wait 'til my friends hear what Jesus did!"

Based on John 6:1-15

Making a Man of God

A MAN OF GOD KNOWS THAT SMALL THINGS BECOME GREAT WHEN JESUS GETS INVOLVED.

When the boy looked at his lunch it didn't seem like very much—just some bread and fish. But when he shared his food with Jesus, it turned into a huge picnic! Jesus can take what we give him—no matter how small—and make it something great.

Can you do something for Jesus? How about sharing something you have with someone else? Or cheering someone up when they are sad. Maybe you can visit someone who is lonely. Or give someone a hug.

Those are pretty simple things, right? But even a simple thing can turn into something very special when we do it for Jesus. Give it a try. You'll see!

Coaching Tips

Have you ever passed up an opportunity to do good because it just didn't seem like you had much to offer? Did it seem that your little bit wouldn't make any difference? Five loaves and two fish didn't seem like much either in the face of a huge hungry crowd.

Make a memory with the boy in your life. Decide together on a simple act of kindness the two of you can do in Jesus' name. Talk about it afterward. How might Jesus use you to show his love and power to someone else?

A Verse to Remember

EVERYTHING IS POSSIBLE WITH GOD.
MARK 10:27

THE RUNAWAY
SON

"When I die," a rich man told his sons, "everything I own will be yours."

But one of his sons was unhappy and impatient. "I want my share now, Father," he said.

When his father gave him the money the boy ran away from home. He was tired of everyone telling him what to do. He wanted to do whatever he pleased.

And that is exactly what he did. He bought anything he wanted and broke all the rules he had been taught. He did all the things he could never do at home.

Before long, the boy had wasted all his money. He had no place to live and nothing to eat, and the only job he could find was feeding pigs. He was so hungry even pig food looked good!

"I wish I were home," groaned the boy. "My father's servants live better than this."

But he was ashamed of what he had done and afraid
to go home. Wouldn't his father be angry?

"Maybe Father will let me be one of his workers,"
he thought. "At least I won't starve."

He headed for home. When he got close, his
father ran to meet him and happily hugged him.
"Welcome home, Son!"

"I don't deserve to be your son," the boy said sadly. "I know I disappointed you. It was wrong to do what I did. I'm so sorry, Father."

"I forgive you," beamed his father. "I'm so happy you're home I'm going to throw a party!"

What a celebration they had!

Based on Luke 15:11-24

Making a Man of God

The runaway boy found out that breaking the rules wasn't a good way to live. Doing wrong things made him feel ashamed. It took courage to ask his father to forgive him.

Are you sometimes afraid to admit it when you break the rules? Just like the father in the story, God is always ready to forgive you. All you have to do is pray and ask him.

Coaching Tips

Tell about a time when you asked for God's forgiveness. How did you feel before you asked forgiveness? How did you feel afterward? Let your young man know that you love him no matter what and that you are always ready to forgive him when he asks. Asking your young man for forgiveness when you do something to hurt him will set a powerful example!

A Verse to Remember

IF WE CONFESS OUR SINS TO HIM, HE IS FAITHFUL AND JUST TO FORGIVE US AND TO CLEANSE US FROM EVERY WRONG.
1 JOHN 1:9

THE GOOD NEIGHBOR

One day a man was traveling down the road when he was attacked by a gang. They stole his money and they took his clothes. Then they beat the man up and left him lying beside the road. He was hurt so badly he was barely alive!

A little while later, a priest came by on his way to the next town. As he got closer, the priest could tell that the man was hurt. But he didn't want to get too close, so he crossed to the other side of the road and kept going.

After a while, a helper in God's house walked down
the same road. When he saw the man who had been
beaten, he went over to look at him. The poor man
looked awful! But the helper didn't want to get
involved, so he crossed the road and hurried away.

Then a stranger came by, a man from another country. When he saw the man lying by the road, he felt very bad. He climbed off his donkey and began to take care of the man. He bandaged the man's cuts. Then the stranger put the man on his donkey and took him to a small hotel where he could rest and get well.

"Here's some money," the stranger told the hotel manager. "If it costs more than that, I will pay you when I come back."

When he was sure the man would be okay, the stranger went on his way.

Based on Luke 10

Making a Man of God

A MAN OF GOD HELPS
PEOPLE IN NEED.

Why didn't the first two men
stop to help the man who was
hurt? Do you think they were
afraid? Were they too busy or
in a hurry? What if they didn't
know the man? Maybe they
didn't know first aid! Or maybe
they thought someone else
would help.

What do you do when you
see people who need help?

What would you do if Jesus
needed help? Remember that
Jesus wants us to treat others
the same way we would treat
him.

Coaching Tips

Tell a real-life story or two about helping. Has someone reached out to you in some practical way when you were sick, hurt, stranded, broke, in trouble, etc.? What did that help mean to you? Perhaps you've had an opportunity to lend a hand when someone else was in need. How did it make you feel?

Look for a way that your young man can join you in offering tangible assistance to someone in need. Make certain that he understands that he is not "earning points" with you (or with God) by doing good deeds!

A Verse to Remember

LOVE YOUR NEIGHBOR AS YOURSELF.
LUKE 10:27

ONE
OUT OF TEN

Ten men had a terrible disease called leprosy. No one was allowed to touch them—not even their families. Everyone was afraid of catching the disease!

"Jesus is coming to town," said one of the men. "I hear that he can heal people."

"Do you think he can cure leprosy?" asked another man.

"I don't know," said the first man. "Why don't we ask him and find out?"

So the ten men waited for Jesus to arrive. They were excited because of the wonderful things they had heard about him. But they were also nervous. What if Jesus wouldn't look at them or talk to them?

When Jesus finally entered the town, the men weren't allowed to get close to him because of their disease. How would he ever see them? They started yelling at the top of their lungs. "Jesus, please help us!"

Jesus looked at them. "Go show yourselves to the priest," he said.

In those days a priest had to check people out to see if they had the disease. But what would the priest say?

So they started off to find a priest, but as they were walking each of them realized that their disease had completely disappeared!

One of the men turned around and ran right up to Jesus. "I'm healed!" he said. "Praise God!" Then he bowed down at Jesus' feet crying, "Thank you! Thank you!"

"Didn't I heal ten men?" asked Jesus. "Where are the others?"

The other nine men never returned to thank Jesus.

Based on
Luke 17:11-19

Making a Man of God

A MAN OF GOD IS THANKFUL.

Life must have been awful for the poor men with leprosy. But when Jesus healed them, they could go back to their families and friends and live a normal life again. They had a lot to be thankful for.

What are you thankful for? Your family? Your friends? Can you think of some other things to be thankful for?

Do you ever forget to say thank you to others? To God? Why not tell him now?

Coaching Tips

Explain how it feels to do something for someone, and receive no thanks in return. Relate that to how God must feel when we take his goodness for granted.

Model thankfulness by offering your own list of things (including relationships) for which you are thankful. Emphasize that we should be thankful for small things as well as big things.

A Verse to Remember

GIVE THANKS TO THE LORD
FOR HE IS GOOD.
PSALM 107:1

LITTLE MAN,
BIG HEART

Zacchaeus was a very rich man. But he wasn't very honest, and he didn't have very many friends. Most of the people he knew thought he was a terrible man.

When Jesus came to town, lots of people crowded around him. Zacchaeus had heard about Jesus and he wanted to see him, too. But Zacchaeus wasn't very tall. He couldn't see Jesus at all.

I know what I'll do, he thought. He looked around for a tree. When he found one close to the road, he climbed up in it. Now he could see Jesus just fine!

When Jesus walked by, he looked up in the tree and saw Zacchaeus. "Zacchaeus," he said. "Come down right away. I want to come to your house to visit you."

Zacchaeus could hardly believe his ears. Jesus, the great teacher, wanted to come to his house! And he even called him by name!

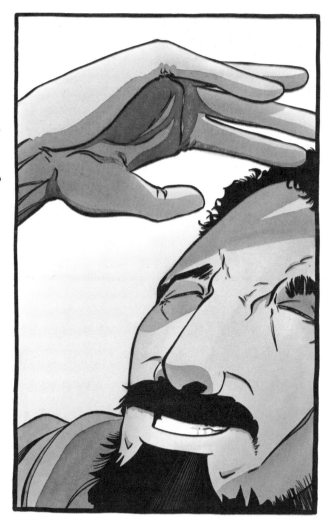

Zacchaeus was so excited he couldn't wait. He climbed right down and took Jesus to his house.

Zacchaeus' neighbors were not very happy about this. "Why would Jesus go home with such a rotten person?" they grumbled.

But something wonderful was happening to Zacchaeus. As soon as he was with Jesus, he began to change.

"I will give half of my money to the poor," he told Jesus. "And I will pay back everyone that I have cheated–four times as much!"

"Today you have become part of God's family," said Jesus.

Based on Luke 19

Making a Man of God

A MAN OF GOD FOLLOWS JESUS.

Zacchaeus wanted to see Jesus so badly that he climbed a tree! And once he met Jesus, he was never the same again. He didn't want to do bad things anymore. In fact, he wanted to do good things to help people.

Do you want to follow Jesus? Can you think of ways to spend time with him?

Coaching Tips

Explain that even though we can't be physically close to Jesus, we can still spend time with him by praying and by reading what he has to say in the Bible. The more time we spend with Jesus, the more our attitudes and behaviors are likely to reflect his values, and that's what following him is all about.

Why not spend some time together with your young man, learning about Jesus' life and teachings?

Open yourself up to his way of thinking. It will change the way you live, just as it changed Zacchaeus.

A Verse to Remember

FOLLOW GOD'S EXAMPLE IN EVERYTHING YOU DO.

EPHESIANS 5:1

The
MASTER'S
MONEY

A rich man was getting ready to go on a long trip.
"While I'm gone I want you to take care of my
money," he told his servants.

He gave one servant five bags of money. To
another servant he gave two bags. Finally, he gave
the last servant one bag. Then he left on his trip.

After a long time, the rich man came back home. He called his servants together again. He wanted to see what they had done with his money.

"Sir, you gave me five bags of money," said the first servant. "I used the money to make some more, and now I have ten bags."

"Good job," said his master. "I will give you a more important job. Let's have a party to celebrate!"

"Sir," said the next servant. "You gave me two bags. I used the money wisely, and now I have four bags."

"That's great!" said his master. "I will give you a more important job, too. Let's celebrate together!"

Last came the servant with one bag of money. "Sir, I was afraid of you," he said. "I didn't want to lose your money. So I dug a hole in the ground and buried it." He held up one bag. "Here it is."

"You are a bad, lazy servant," said the master. "You should have put my money in the bank, at least. Then it would have earned some interest."

Then the master took away his money and got rid of him.

Based on Matthew 25

Making a Man of God

A MAN OF GOD WORKS HARD.

The first two servants took what their master gave them. They used the money to make even more money. That took a lot of work, but their master was happy. Why was the master unhappy with the last servant?

God is like the master. He gives us things, too. Can you think of things God gives us? What can you do to take care of the things God has given you?

Coaching Tips

Help your young man to think beyond the material things he has been blessed with. What other things can he name that come from God, and how can he care for them as well? Tell him about the things you have received from God's hand.

It is important to note that the servants in the story were rewarded for their diligence, not for what they started out with. Some people are accountable for more than others. How are you doing with what you've been given?

A Verse to Remember

WORK HARD AND BECOME A LEADER; BE
LAZY AND BECOME A SLAVE.
PROVERBS 12:24

CLEANING UP
GOD'S HOUSE

One day when Jesus was visiting the city, he decided to go to God's house. Many people were there to worship God. Some came from far away. They came because it was a special holiday for God's people.

In those days God's people
brought their best animals
(like sheep, calves, or doves) to offer to God. This was
a way to worship him. So when Jesus went inside, he
wasn't surprised by all the noise he heard.

But what he saw made him very sad and angry.
People weren't just there to worship. Some of
them were buying and selling animals. Others
were trading money with people from faraway
places. Instead of looking like God's house, it
looked like a big market!

"Get these things out of here," Jesus said.
"Don't turn my Father's house into a marketplace!"

Before anyone knew what was happening, Jesus took some rope and made a whip. He began to chase out the people who were buying and selling, along with their animals. People ran in every direction to get away from him. Then Jesus went to where the people were trading money. He turned over their tables and threw their money on the floor.

"This is supposed to be a house of prayer," he said, "but you have turned it into a place to cheat people."

"Who said you could do this?" asked the leaders of the people. They didn't like Jesus. They didn't believe that he was the Son of God.

Based on John 2

Making a Man of God

A MAN OF GOD SHOWS
RESPECT FOR GOD.

Why do you think Jesus was upset
when he went into God's house?
The buyers and sellers spent a lot
of time in God's house. Do you
think they were showing respect
for God? Why not?

Is God's house the only place
you need to show respect for God?
Can you think of some ways to
show him respect?

Coaching Tips

It is all too easy to think that following a certain set of rules is the way to show our respect for God. But God is more interested in the attitude of our hearts than he is in hollow acts of reverence. Respectful attitudes will lead to reverential acts.

Encourage your young man to adopt an attitude of respect for his Heavenly Father.

A Verse to Remember

HOLY, HOLY, HOLY IS THE LORD ALMIGHTY.
ISAIAH 6:3

WASHING
DIRTY FEET

Jesus and his closest friends were about to have a very special dinner when Jesus got up from the table and took off his robe. He wrapped a towel around his waist. Then he took a large bowl and poured water into it.

What is Jesus doing? his friends wondered.

Jesus carried the bowl of water to where one of his friends was sitting. He knelt down and set the bowl on the floor. Then he took off the man's sandals and began to wash the dust from his feet. When he had finished, he took the towel from around his waist and carefully dried them.

Jesus picked up the bowl, went to the next man, and began to do the same thing all over again.

This is a servant's job, thought his friends. This isn't something the Son of God should do!

But Jesus just kept washing feet, all around the room until he came to Peter.

"Why do you want to wash my feet?" asked Peter. He didn't look very happy about it.

"Someday you will understand why I am doing this," answered Jesus.

"No!" said Peter. "You will never wash my feet."

"If I don't wash you," said Jesus, "you won't belong to me."

"Well in that case, wash my hands and my head too."

When Jesus was finished, he put his robe back on and sat down to eat. "I have given you an example to follow," he told his friends. "Do as I have done to you."

Based on John 13

Making a Man of God

A MAN OF GOD SERVES OTHERS.

Jesus was a very important person, the most important person in the whole world. And most important people expect others to serve them. But Jesus was different. He wasn't too proud to serve others. And by his example, he showed us that serving is for everyone, no matter how important you are.

Can you follow Jesus' example? You may not wash anyone's feet, but there are many ways to serve. Can you think of a way to serve someone? Who will you serve today?

Coaching Tips

Serving is important. And God promises to bless us in our serving. But if we serve in order to be praised or recognized, we are only serving ourselves. Show your young man how to serve others quietly and sincerely. At the same time, however, be sure to encourage him whenever you "catch" him in the act of serving.

A Verse to Remember

SERVE EACH OTHER
IN HUMILITY.
1 PETER 5:5

A ONE-MAN PARADE

Jesus walked with his friends on the road to the city. He sent two of them into a little town along the way. "You will see a colt that has never been ridden," he told them. "Untie it and bring it here."

Of course, they found the colt just as Jesus said they would. But the colt's owners wanted to know what they were doing with it. "Jesus needs it," they said.

So the owners let them have the colt and they brought it to Jesus. Then they took off their coats and put them on the colt's back. That way Jesus would be more comfortable.

Jesus was very famous and soon a crowd gathered to see him riding into the city. Many people spread out their coats on the road in front of the colt. Others added soft leafy branches. It all made a kind of carpet for Jesus to ride on. People shouted and sang, telling about the miracles they had seen. They said wonderful things about Jesus.

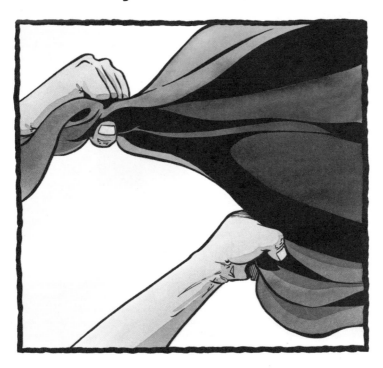

"Bless the king who comes in the name of
the Lord!" they said. "Glory in the highest
heaven!"

Some people didn't like all the fuss. "Tell
your followers to stop praising you like
this," they told Jesus.

But Jesus wouldn't listen to them. "If they keep quiet," he said, "the stones along the road will start cheering."

The parade went on and on. The people treated Jesus like a hero for all the miracles he had done.

Based on Luke 19

Making a Man of God

A MAN OF GOD WORSHIPS
JESUS AS THE SON OF GOD.

The people in the crowd had many different reasons to praise Jesus. Some were excited because he healed people. Maybe they knew about his other miracles, too. And some probably thought he was a great teacher. Others thought he would be their king and rule their country.

Do you worship Jesus? What is the most important thing about him?

Coaching Tips

Jesus is many things: a healer, a miracle-worker, a teacher, our friend and our leader. But your young man may need help to see that Jesus' words and deeds demonstrate that he is more than just a great man; he is the Son of God. That means he can do anything, he knows everything-in short, he is God, just as he claimed. If we worship him as something less than that, we are not really worshiping him at all.

A Verse to Remember

YOU REALLY ARE THE SON OF GOD!
MATTHEW 14:33

THE GREATEST LOVE

The leaders of the people didn't like the things Jesus said. They wanted to get rid of him. So they made up lies about him and brought him to the governor.

"What has he done?" asked the governor.

"He is a criminal," said the leaders. "Give him the death penalty."

"I don't think he has done anything bad," said the governor. But the leaders wouldn't give up. Finally the governor agreed to put Jesus to death.

Soldiers took Jesus and beat him with a whip. They made a crown of thorns and put it on his head. They spit on him and hit him and made fun of him.

Then they took Jesus to a hill outside the city. They nailed his hands and feet to a rough wooden cross, and waited for him to die.

Jesus looked down from the cross at the people who had treated him so cruelly. "Father," he prayed, "forgive these people, because they don't know what they are doing."

Two criminals were hanging beside Jesus. One of them said, "We deserve to die for the bad things we did. But Jesus didn't do anything wrong." Then he asked Jesus to take him to heaven.

"Today you will be with me in Paradise," said Jesus.

When Jesus saw his mother standing nearby, he was very sad. So he asked his friend John to take care of her.

"It is finished," Jesus said at last, and he bowed his head and died.

Based on Luke 23 and John 19

Making a Man of God

A MAN OF GOD UNDERSTANDS THAT
EVERYONE MATTERS TO GOD.

Jesus didn't die because he did anything
bad. He died to take the punishment for
the bad things people do. You are so
important to him that he died for
you, too.

Can you tell who is important to Jesus
in the story?

Some people are different from you.
Some people do things you don't like. Are
they important to Jesus? Are they
important to you, too?

Coaching Tips

Does your circle of friends include people whose gender, religion, race, culture, or social status is different? How do you deal with the "difficult people" in your life-the ones that get under your skin? Do you look out for the welfare of others, even when under pressure? Your example in this area will speak volumes.

Remember that God doesn't play favorites. The gift of God's grace is available to all-no matter who they are or what they have done!

A Verse to Remember

Christ died for everyone.
2 Corinthians 5:14

SURPRISE
IN THE
GARDEN

When Jesus died on the cross, his friends were very sad. They were scared, too. They didn't know what to do without Jesus.

Early one morning, one of his friends, Mary Magdalene, went to the garden where Jesus was buried.

It was still kind of dark out, but Mary could see that the grave was open. Someone had moved the stone away from it!

What's going on? she wondered as she looked inside. Jesus was nowhere to be seen. Only his clothes were there.

Mary felt very confused. Who would take Jesus away? And where would they take him? She began to cry.

When she looked back inside the grave, she could hardly believe her eyes. Two angels were sitting there, dressed in shiny white robes!

"Why are you crying," they asked.

"Someone took Jesus away," she answered. "I don't know where he is."

"Why are you crying?" asked a gentle voice behind her. "Who are you looking for?"

She looked over her shoulder and saw a man standing there. She didn't recognize him, so she thought he was the gardener.

"Tell me where you have put Jesus and I will go get him," she said.

"Mary!" said the man.

As soon as she heard her name, Mary turned around. It was Jesus! He was alive again, just as he promised he would be! She ran to hug him. She could hardly wait to tell all his friends. Jesus was alive!

Based on John 20

Making a Man of God

A MAN OF GOD TRUSTS JESUS TO
KEEP HIS PROMISES.

People promise things almost every day. But sometimes people don't keep their promises, do they? Has anyone ever made a promise to you? Did he keep it?

Jesus died to take the punishment for the bad things we do. But he promised to come back to life so we could be friends with God. Did he keep his promise?

If he can keep a promise that big, he can keep any promise!

Coaching Tips

Talk about some other promises that Jesus made. Following are a few suggestions: Whoever believes in him will have eternal life (John 3:16); He will be with you always (Matthew 28:20); He will take care of you (Matthew 6:32, 33).

Nothing can compare to the trustworthiness of Jesus. But taking care to keep your promises just might help your young man learn to trust his heavenly Father.

A Verse to Remember

HE ALWAYS DOES JUST
WHAT HE SAYS.
1 CORINTHIANS 1:9

FORGOTTEN

When Jesus came back to life some of his friends and followers could hardly believe that he was alive.

"I won't believe it unless I can touch him," said Thomas.

"Maybe he's just a ghost," said another friend.

But Jesus came to visit them again and again for forty days. He wanted to prove that he was really alive. He let Thomas touch the scars in his hands and side. He traveled with two of his friends to another town. He helped Peter, John, and some other men catch a boat full of fish. He ate meals with them. And he taught them more about God.

One day when Jesus was with his friends,
they asked him to tell them about the
future.

"That's not for you to know," he said.
"But the Holy Spirit will give you power to
tell people about me everywhere."

Then, while his friends watched, Jesus rose up into the clouds where they couldn't see him anymore. They looked until their eyes hurt, but Jesus was gone!

What's going on? they wondered. Where did he go? They were amazed, scared and sad all at the same time.

Jesus was their very best friend, their teacher, their leader. He died on the cross for their sins and came back to life. But now he was gone!

Suddenly, two men in white robes appeared. "Why are you staring at the sky?" they asked. "Jesus has gone to heaven. And someday he will come back again!"

Based on Acts 1

Making a Man of God

A MAN OF GOD HAS HOPE.

When Jesus was on the earth he told his friends that he was going to go to heaven to make a home ready for them. He wanted them to come live where he lives. He wants you to live with him someday, too. Isn't that something to look forward to?

Can you imagine what heaven is like? Can you imagine what it would be like to see Jesus and talk to him? What would you like to say to him?

Coaching Tips

There are lots of things we don't know about the future. We don't know when Jesus will return, and we don't know all the details about what will happen. But don't let that discourage you or your young man. Our hope is in Jesus—and he is coming back! In the meanwhile, since he is busy making a home for us, let's be busy working for him.

A Verse to Remember

WHEN EVERYTHING IS READY, I WILL COME AND GET YOU.
JOHN 14:3

JUST THE FACTS, PLEASE

After Jesus returned to heaven, many people believed the Good News about him. They got together at each other's homes to learn more about Jesus and to pray. They wanted to share everything they had.

Some people sold their land and brought the money to the church leaders.

The leaders gave the money to the poor so that everyone had enough food and clothing.

A man named Ananias came to see Peter. "I sold some land," Ananias said. "Now I want to give all the money to the church to help the poor."

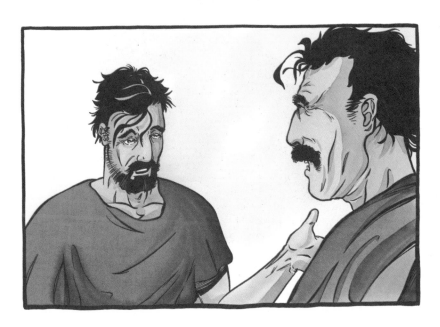

But Ananias wasn't telling the whole truth. He was only giving part of the money to the church.

"Why are you lying?" asked Peter. "You can do what you want with your property-you can keep it or sell it. And you can give away the money if you want. But you kept some for yourself, didn't you?"

Ananias didn't answer. He just fell down dead on the spot.

A little while later, Ananias' wife, Sapphira, came to see Peter. She had no idea what had happened to her husband.

"How much money did you get when you sold your land?" Peter asked her.

Sapphira told him the same thing that Ananias had said.

Then Peter said "Why did you and your husband agree to lie about this? You haven't just lied to us. You have lied to God!"

And just like her husband, Sapphira fell down dead. And everyone who heard about it was afraid.

Based on Acts 5

Making a Man of God

A MAN OF GOD TELLS THE TRUTH.

Ananias and Sapphira could have done anything they wanted with the money they earned. No one would have minded if they had given some of the money to the church and kept some for themselves. Why do you think they lied about the money?

Have you ever said something that wasn't true? Ask God to help you always tell the truth!

Coaching Tips

We like to put a "spin" on our lies in order to feel less guilty, don't we? "It was just a little white lie," we say. "It didn't hurt anyone." Or, "It wasn't exactly a lie. I just left out a few key facts." But anything we do or say to create a false impression is dishonest.

Your young man watches and listens to what you say and do. Will he learn to tell the truth, the whole truth, and nothing but the truth?

A Verse to Remember

Don't lie to each other.
Colossians 3:9

Outdoor
SCHOOL

Philip was a leader in the church. He was busy telling people about Jesus when an angel came to see him. "Go down the road toward the sea," said the angel. God had a job for him to do. So Philip left what he was doing and started down the road.

Along the way, he saw a man, riding in his
carriage, reading. Philip could see that this
man was from Africa, and that he was a very
important man. In fact, the man was in charge
of all of his government's money! When Philip
got closer, he could hear the man reading out
loud. He was reading God's Word!

Philip ran up beside him. "Do you understand what you are reading?" he asked the man.

The man looked down from where he was sitting. "How can I understand it when I don't have anyone to teach me?" he said. "Can you help me?"

When Philip said yes, the African man invited him to climb up in the carriage. Then Philip began to explain God's Word. He answered the man's questions. Then he told him the Good News about Jesus.

The farther they traveled, and the more Philip explained, the more the African man understood. It wasn't long before he believed the Good News and trusted in Jesus.

"Look! There is some water over there," said the man. "I would like to follow Jesus' example and be baptized. May I?"

So Philip took him down to the water and baptized him.

Based on Acts 8

Making a Man of God

A MAN OF GOD IS ALWAYS
READY TO LEARN.

The man from Africa was a very important man. He was probably very rich, too. But he wanted to learn about God. And he wasn't too proud to ask someone to teach him.

Some people think they know enough about God already. They don't think they need to learn any more. Do you think they are right?

Who teaches you about God? Do you want to learn more?

Coaching Tips

Learning about God and his ways is the most important learning your young man can engage in. You can play a key role in his learning by taking him to church regularly, by exposing him to God's Word, even by doing what you are doing right now!

A young man learns, too, by asking questions. Answer each one with care. And remember that he looks up to you. What is he learning through your example?

A Verse to Remember

TEACH ME YOUR WAYS, O LORD.
PSALM 86:11

THE GREAT ESCAPE

Peter and his friends told everyone the good news about Jesus. But that made the king angry. He didn't want them to talk about Jesus. He sent soldiers to arrest Peter and put him in jail. Peter was chained to two soldiers, one on each side. More soldiers were outside. They didn't want him to get away.

When Peter's friends found out where he was, they were afraid that he would be killed. So they gathered together and began to pray that God would keep him safe.

One night, after Peter had fallen asleep, an angel appeared. Bright light flooded the jail cell and Peter's chains fell off.

"Get up, quick!" said the angel, nudging Peter awake. "Get dressed and follow me."

Peter thought he was having some kind of dream, but he did what the angel said. Soon they were outside, walking right past the guards, through the gates, and into the street. Suddenly the angel disappeared.

Now Peter knew he wasn't dreaming. "It's true," he said to himself. "God sent the angel to rescue me from the king." So he hurried to a friend's house.

Inside the house, people were praying. A young girl came to the door when Peter knocked.

"Peter is at the door," she told his friends.

"No way," they said. "You must be crazy!"

Peter kept knocking at the door, and when they finally let him in, they could hardly believe their eyes. God had answered their prayers. Peter was safe.

Based on Acts 12

Making a Man of God

A MAN OF GOD KEEPS PRAYING,
NO MATTER WHAT.

We don't know how long Peter's friends were praying, but it must have been a long time. Do you think they were surprised when Peter escaped from jail?

Do you think God answers when you pray? Do you pray for big things or little things? Do you pray for other people, or just for yourself?

Coaching Tips

God hears our prayers and he always answers. But that doesn't mean that he always says "yes." Like a good parent, sometimes he says "no," and sometimes he says "wait a while." Only he knows what is best for us.

Peter's friends didn't know what to expect from God, but they didn't give up. They kept praying until they got an answer–even though the answer surprised them!

A Verse to Remember

KEEP ON PRAYING.

1 THESSALONIANS 5:17

SINGING IN JAIL

Paul and Silas traveled from place to place telling people about Jesus. Some people listened and believed them. But others didn't like what they said at all.

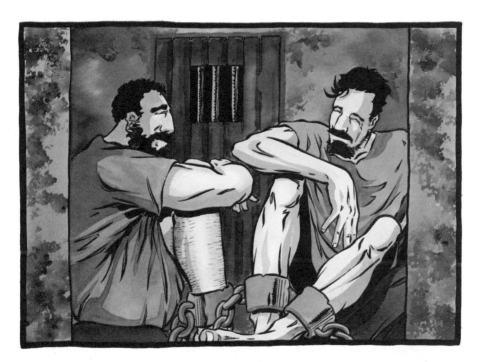

One day some people got very upset. "Paul and Silas are causing trouble," they told the leaders of their city. "They are teaching things we don't believe."

So the leaders made Paul and Silas take off their robes and they beat them with sticks. Then they threw them in jail! "Make sure these men don't escape!" they warned the jailer.

Just to make sure, the jailer put chains on their feet so they couldn't walk.

In the middle of the night, Paul and Silas prayed that God would help them. Then they sang worship songs so loud that everyone in the jail could hear them.

All of a sudden, the jail started shaking. It was an earthquake! The chains fell off the prisoners and the jail doors flew wide open.

The jailer was scared. If his boss found out that
the prisoners had run away, he would be in big
trouble. He might even be killed!

"Don't worry, sir!" called Paul. "We're still here."
The jailer could hardly believe it! Why would these
men stay when they could run away? Maybe what
they said about Jesus was true, after all.

"I want to know Jesus," he said. "Will you tell me how?"

So Paul and Silas told him the good news about Jesus, and he believed. Then he took them to his house and took care of them.

Based on Acts 16:16-40

Making a Man of God

A MAN OF GOD SHARES THE
GOOD NEWS BY DOING WHAT
JESUS WOULD DO.

The people in that city didn't treat Paul
and Silas very well, did they? If Paul
and Silas had run away, who would
have told the jailer the good news? He
could tell just by the way they acted
that they knew Jesus. And that's why
he wanted to know more about it.

Do you know Jesus? Acting the way
he wants you to-even when people
aren't nice to you-shows others that
Jesus is with you. Remember that
Jesus will help you do the right thing.
Just ask him!

Coaching Tips

Remember the old saying, "actions speak louder than words"? It is far easier to talk about faith than it is to practice it, but words fall on deaf ears unless they are backed up by action. Explain what it means to "walk the talk," then demonstrate it consistently for the young man in your life. He'll want to be just like you!

A Verse to Remember

Let your good deeds shine out for all to see, so that everyone will praise your heavenly Father.
Matthew 5:16